Rainy day ideas

M. Madeleine Mays
Rainy day ideas

Cover illustration by Alan Cracknell
Text illustrations by the author

A Piccolo original
Pan Books Ltd London and Sydney

First published 1975 by Pan Books Ltd,
Cavaye Place, London SW10 9PG
ISBN 0 330 24355 1
© M. Madeleine Mays 1975

Printed in Great Britain by
Richard Clay (The Chaucer Press) Ltd, Bungay, Suffolk

Introduction

If it's pouring with rain and you're stuck indoors wondering what to do, look in this book and you'll find lots of ideas for making all kinds of funny, pretty and useful things. And you won't have to stretch your pocket-money in the process! As you can see from the list of suggested 'ingredients' below, most of the things you'll need can be found easily enough around the house.

Ingredients
All kinds of paper — flimsy, stiff, coloured, plain white, greaseproof, corrugated, tissue, crepe
Postcards
Cellophane, tin-foil cases
Magazines
Scissors, hole-puncher
Sticky tape, glue
String, twine, cotton thread, lengths of wool, ribbons
Ruler, compasses, set-square
Pencils, felt-tip pens, paint-brushes, crayons, waterproof inks
All kinds of paints — household, oils, water colours
Pins, paper clips, paper-fasteners
Rubber bands
Straws
Pieces of material, plain and patterned
Cotton reels
Beads and buttons of all shapes and sizes
Pieces of wood, small nails, fuse wire
Matchboxes and matchsticks
Empty cartons of all shapes and sizes
Cardboard tubes from toilet rolls, kitchen towels, etc
Twigs, shells
Dried beans, uncooked rice

Suitable Containers

As you gather together the things you will be needing, it's a good idea to find containers for them, so that you can keep them tidy until you're ready to use them.

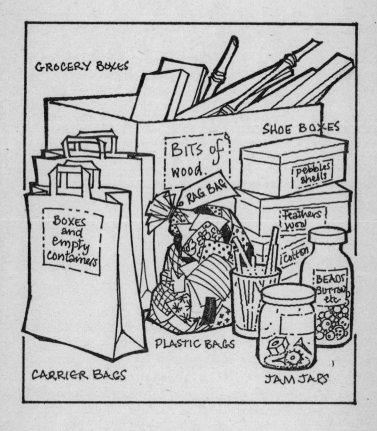

Keep everything in a special corner and label the containers neatly.

Seven (?) Dwarfs

Use the cardboard tube from a toilet roll, or any other suitable tube or round container.

1 Glue on coloured paper or paint it all over.

2 Trace figure A (on the opposite page) onto paper, colour it and cut the hair along the broken lines. Glue the strip round the top of the tube.

3 Cut soft paper, such as tissue or crepe, or cloth, about 15 cm by 12 cm. Fold up 2·5 cm along the bottom. Bend it round to fit over the top of the tube, glue up the side join, and tie in a bunch near the top.

4 Cut fringed paper for beards. Glue on.

For the belt use paper, tape or ribbon, and if possible a small buckle from an old sandal, or draw it on. Feet are cut from black paper and glued under the rim of the tube. You can add arms as shown, or not, as you like.

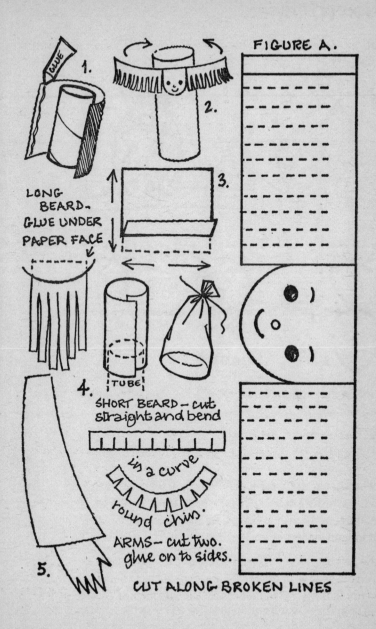

FIGURE A.

1.

2.

3.

LONG
BEARD -
GLUE UNDER
PAPER FACE

4. TUBE

SHORT BEARD — cut
straight and bend

in a curve

round chin.

ARMS — cut two.
glue on to sides.

5.

CUT ALONG BROKEN LINES

Fir-cone birds

Owl Choose one large and one small fir-cone, the small one if possible with part of the stem still attached to look like a beak. Glue them together as shown at A, using a strong glue. When the glue is dry, cut 2 small bits of matchstick to glue on for legs. Arrange them so it will sit firmly balanced on a triangular shape made by the top end of the cone and the legs, as shown at B. Cut 2 tiny bits of match to glue on for ears and 2 small beads for eyes.

Stand your owls on the mantelpiece or glue a couple to a small twig.

Chicken Find one large and one small fir-cone. Glue them together in position as shown at A. Leave to dry till the glue hardens.

Twist a piece of wire into 2 legs with round flat shapes for feet, as at C. Wind the ends round the body between the 'scales' to fix the legs in place. Add a dab of glue. When dry, move the legs into a position so the bird stands up.

If you can find a few small feathers, glue one to the head and several in place for a tail.

Glue on two small beads or sequins for eyes, or use drawing-pins.

Slice a bit of match diagonally (B). Glue into the end of small cone for a beak.

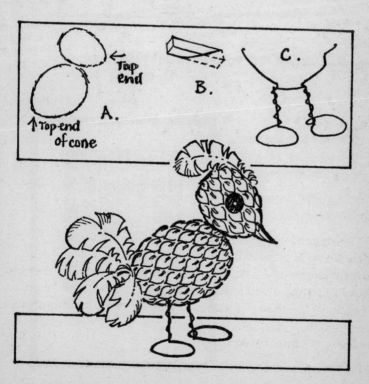

Old stamps for decoration

If you have an old picture frame, make an original wall decoration by sticking the prettiest stamps you can find onto paper cut to fit the frame.

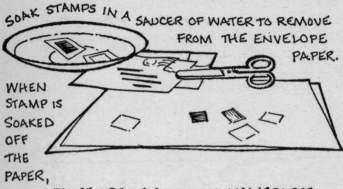

SOAK STAMPS IN A SAUCER OF WATER TO REMOVE FROM THE ENVELOPE PAPER.

WHEN STAMP IS SOAKED OFF THE PAPER,

PLACE UPSIDE-DOWN ON NEWSPAPER TO DRY.

Rule a few very pale lines with a ruler and set-square as guide-lines for your arrangement.

You can then fix them on with stamp-hinges or glue.

Brighten up an old lampshade like this.

Collect some ordinary stamps, not the special ones you want for your stamp album, as you will have to use glue and not stamp-hinges for this one.

Soak, remove from the envelopes and dry as before. When dry, press them flat under a heavy weight such as a big book, if necessary.

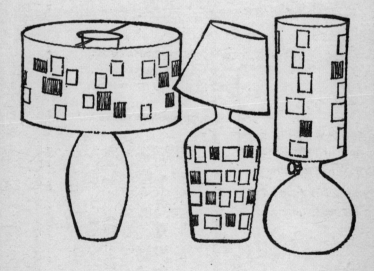

Glue an arrangement onto a plain lampshade, or onto the base if it's a suitable one.

If you have some clear varnish paint it over the stamps.

Make a pin-cushion

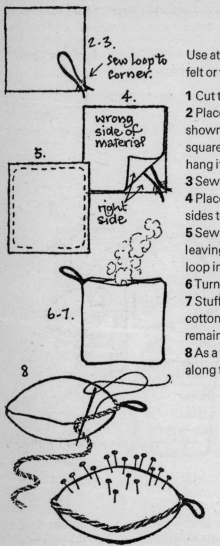

2.3.
Sew loop to corner.

4.
wrong side of material

5.

right side

6-7.

8

Use attractive scraps of material — felt or velvet look very good.

1 Cut two squares.
2 Place a loop of tape or braid, as shown, on the right side of one square, if you will be wanting to hang it up.
3 Sew it to the corner.
4 Place the other square on top, right sides together.
5 Sew round the edge of the squares, leaving a small gap and securing the loop in place as you go.
6 Turn right side out.
7 Stuff with kapok, foam rubber, cotton wool, etc. Sew up the remaining slit.
8 As a finishing touch, sew braid along the seam.

Make yourself a hat

Use a large, round cottage-cheese, ice-cream or other similar plastic container.

If there is lettering on it you can either scrape it off or paint over it.

CUT THIS PART OUT

Hold the container upside-down in the middle of a piece of cardboard and draw round it.

Draw a bigger circle outside it for the edge of the hat brim and cut round it.

Draw a smaller circle inside the first one and cut it out. Cut slits from this circle to the next, and slip the card over the carton, bending the flaps up. Glue them to the carton. Tie ribbon round to hide them. Decorate the hat any way you like, with feathers, flowers, etc.

15

Jumping jester

FOR A LARGER FIGURE DRAW THE PARTS YOURSELF INSTEAD OF TRACING~

1 Trace the head and body of the jester on the opposite page onto thin card or stiff paper in one piece.

2 Trace 2 of each pair of arm and leg pieces, but the second set of each must be turned over so you have a right *and a left* arm and leg.

3 Paint and decorate the pieces. Allow to dry.

4 Use a knitting-needle to poke holes where marked with a small o. Put paper-fasteners through them to join the parts together.

5 Turn him over and attach strong thread to join the arms at the points shown. Do the same with the legs. Tie a long piece of thread from the top one to the bottom one so it hangs down.

6 Fix a loop of thread to the back of the head with sticky tape.

8 Hold the loop or hang it up, and pull the long string with the other hand to make him dance. For greater movement, adjust the length of string between arms and legs accordingly.

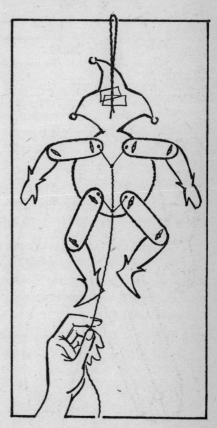

Masks to make

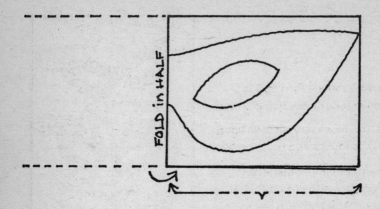

FOLD in HALF

Half the width of paper is same measurement as between nose and ear.

Materials needed
Strong black paper ; ribbon, string or elastic ; and for decoration, feathers, sequins, bristles, bits of fringe, tassels, wool, etc.

Measure from the centre of your nose to your ear and cut a piece of paper twice this length and about 10 cms deep, depending on the design of your mask. Fold it in half across the short width, draw half a mask up to the fold as shown above and cut out through the double thickness. Unfold.

Attach string or ribbon or elastic at the sides to fit round the back of your head, or long enough to tie at the back.

The basic shape as in fig 1 is enough for a highwayman's mask.

You can make up your own fancy mask; some ideas are shown here.

2 Glue feathers along the top.
3 Sew or glue beads round the edge and tie tassels at the sides.
4 Glue a strip of fringing along the bottom.
5 Glue on sequins.
6 Cut a butterfly shape.
7 Draw ears on the basic shape and then cut out. Glue on bristles for whiskers.

1. BASIC MASK

2.

sew on beads

3.

4.

sequins 5.

6. TWO DIFFERENT SHAPES

7.

Tin-foil decorating

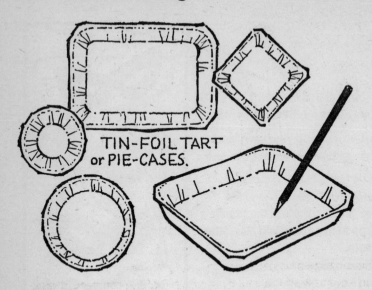

TIN-FOIL TART or PIE-CASES.

1 Save and wash gently any tin-foil pie-, pastry- or tart-cases you can find.
2 Place one of these on the table with a few sheets of paper underneath.
3 With a pencil or used-up biro, draw a design on the smooth base of the foil dish, but don't bend the dish out of shape as you do so.

This will leave the design in the foil which will show up as it catches the light.

OIL-BASED PAINT.

4 You can trace a simple design to use if you like.

If you want to work out your design on paper you can trace it, stick the tracing to the dish with sticky paper, then trace over the design with enough pressure to leave an impression in the foil.

5 If you have any oil-paint or left-over household paint you can colour parts of the picture.

SOME
SIMPLE
IDEAS.

'Stained-glass' windows

Fold a large sheet of greaseproof paper in half and work out your design for *half* a window, the centre on the fold. Use one of the designs on the opposite page or make up your own. Draw it in thick lines with black crayon. Turn the paper over, and lay it on white paper so you can see through to trace the other half onto the second side.

Open it out, clip it to a sheet of black paper and draw over the lines with a biro, pressing heavily enough to leave an impression of the design on the black paper.

Cut away the shapes in the black paper leaving thick black lines between each chunk of space.

Cut brightly coloured cellophane or tissue paper to fit the cut-out spaces, and glue to the back.

Fix the finished design up on a windowpane with sticky tape so the sun shines through.

22

Doll's lamp

1 Use an empty cotton reel. To hide the shape glue cord or string wound neatly round it.

2 Cut some stiff paper to the shape shown.
3 Fold round and glue the straight edges together.

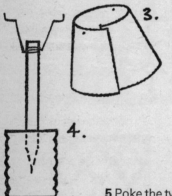

4 Stick a pencil stub into the cotton reel hole and wind a piece of wire round the top in the shape shown.

5 Poke the two wire ends through opposite holes made near the top edges of the shade.

Add pretty braid if you like.

Toy Landscape

If you have some toy farm animals you can make a miniature landscape for them.

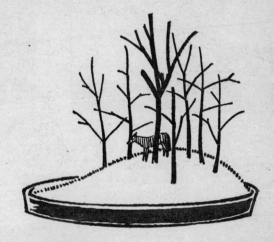

Fill a shallow dish, tray or baking-tray with earth or sand built up on one side into a 'hill'. Find some small twigs and trim them into winter tree-shapes. Stick them into the packed earth, arranging them to look like a wood.

Try and find moss to cover the hill to look like grass before arranging your animals.

Or make a snow-scene : pour a cup of detergent into a small bowl. Add a very little water and whisk till stiff and smooth. Cover the sand with this mixture and arrange the animals as before.

Blowing eggs . . .

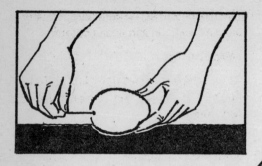

If you want to keep an eggshell for long you have to remove the inside. One way is to eat it — here is another.

Take a raw egg and scrape a small hole in one end with a needle.

Make a hole in the other end about the width of a matchstick.

Put the smaller hole to your lips and gently blow the inside of the egg out of the other end into a bowl.

. . . to decorate

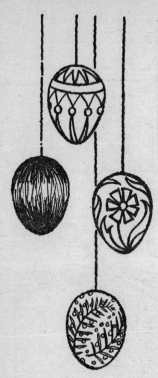

Then paint the egg an attractive colour or paint a design on it in poster colours.

Leave it to dry.

If you do an especially good one and can find a bit of varnish to put over it, it will keep longer.

To hang it up tie a piece of thread to a small bit of matchstick.

Push it lengthwise through the larger hole in the egg and pull taut so it lies across the hole once inside.

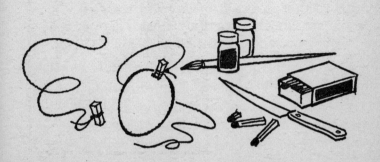

Fabric pictures

string or wool stalks

Use up odd scraps of material to make pictures or designs.

Work out the idea first. Select and cut some plain fabric for the background. Then cut bits of material to the shapes you need, and arrange them on the background material.

Either sew round the edge of each shape, which is best, or use a fabric glue carefully to fix the pieces in position.

You could hang your design on the wall, using the method on the next page, if you allow extra fabric at top and bottom for turn-ups as shown by dotted lines in the illustration above.

Wall hanging

Take a piece of pretty left-over material with a large decorative design.

Cut it into a neat shape.

Turn under the long edges and hem or glue.

Find two thin sticks like bamboo (or 2 knitting-needles would do) a little longer than the width of material.

Turn under the top and bottom edges and sew, making the hems wide enough to slip the sticks through.

Tie a piece of decorative cord to the 2 ends of the stick at the top, and 2 smaller bits to hang down from each end of the one through the bottom.

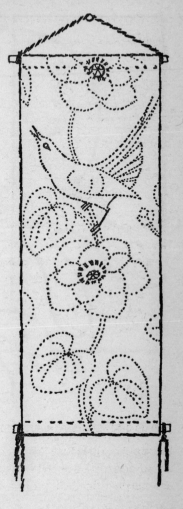

Baby octopus

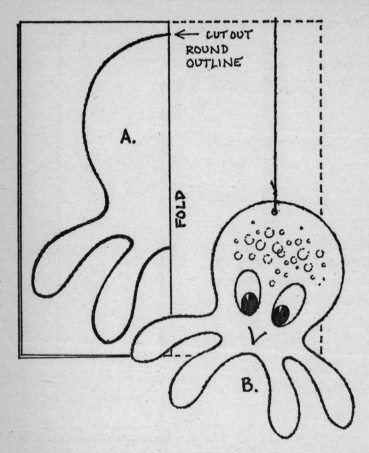

CUT OUT ROUND OUTLINE

A.

FOLD

B.

Take a piece of green card about 9 cm square, or colour some plain card yourself.

Fold in half and trace the shape above marked A onto one side along the fold of the paper.

Cut round the shape through both thicknesses.

Unfold and draw in eyes and mouth.

Make a hole at the top with a pin, thread cotton through, and hang up.

Noughts-and-crosses board

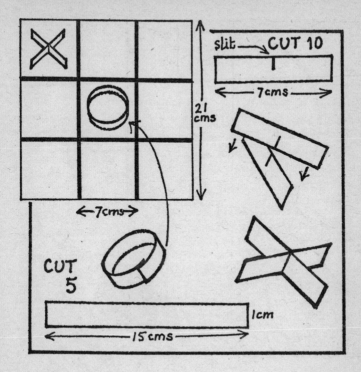

Cut a piece of white card 21 cm square. Measure out 3 squares, 7 cm by 7 cm, each way. Use a dark pencil or felt-tip pen to rule the lines. Colour the squares if you like.

Measure and cut out 5 strips of stiff paper, 15 cm long and 1 cm wide. Bend each one into a circle, overlapping by about 1 cm, and add a dab of glue or sticky tape to hold it together.

Cut out 10 strips 1 cm by 7 cm. Make a cut halfway across the middle of each and fit 2 together by means of the slots till you have 5 crosses.

You can play again and again with these noughts and crosses.

A woolly ball . . .

Cut 2 circles, both the same size, of thin card and cut a small circle out of the centre of each.

Thread a skein of wool through both circles till the centre is packed tight. Use a needle for the last bit. To make it quicker you can wind several strands at once. Use wool all the same colour or different colours.

Cut round the edge, pushing the scissors between the 2 layers of card.

Tie a length of thread or wool round firmly between the circles of card and remove them.

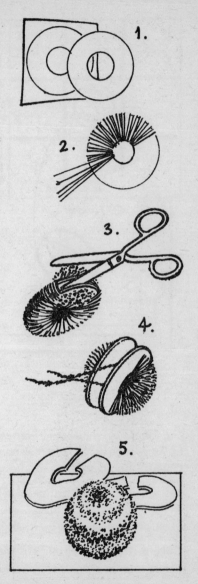

. . . and a woolly owl

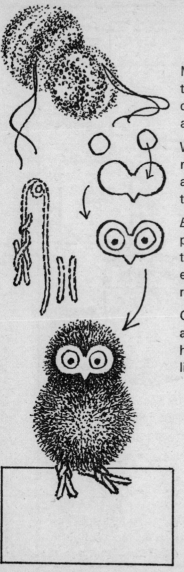

Make two woolly balls as shown on the opposite page. Cut 2 pairs of circles about 5 cm and 7·5 cm across.

When you tie the length of thread round the balls, leave the ends long as you remove the card, and use them to tie the balls firmly together.

Before tying them together twist a piece of pipecleaner or wire round the middle of the biggest ball, so 2 ends stick out for legs. Twist them round 2 small bits for claws.

Cut small bits of felt or paper for eyes and beak, and sew or glue onto the head, pushing them into the wool a little.

A bag to keep things in

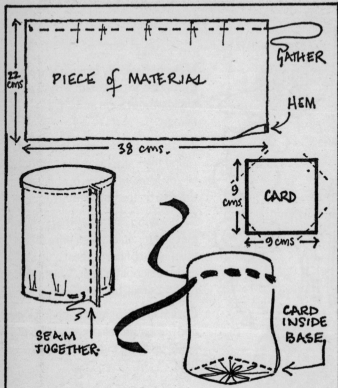

1 Find a piece of material 38 cm by 22 cms and a piece of stiff card 9 cms square. Cut off the corners of the card. Gather the material along one side and stitch a hem along the other.
2 Lay the short edges right sides together and sew up.
3 Turn right side out. Insert card base and draw up gathered edge under it. Fasten off thread. Add a dab of glue under the card if necessary. With a large needle thread very narrow ribbon round near the top.

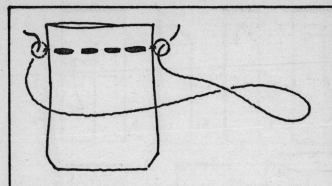

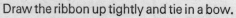

4 Sew a curtain-ring each side on the level of the ribbon but avoiding it. Tie a length of cord or braid to them to hold it by, one end to each ring.
Draw the ribbon up tightly and tie in a bow.

Pop-up greeting card

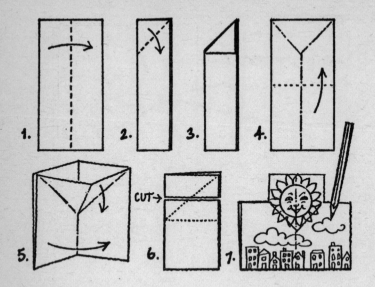

1 Take a piece of paper about 12·5 cm by 25 cm. Fold in half lengthwise.

2, 3 Fold one corner down from the crease along the dotted line. Press this crease firmly, bend the opposite way and crease again.

4 Unfold paper. Fold the bottom half up over the top half along the dotted line.

5 Fold the sides together, pulling the top triangle forward as you do so.

6 Cut off about a quarter of the card from the top. (Dotted line marks the position of the inside fold.)

7 Open out the card and the middle section will pop up. Draw the design shown on the card, or make up your own. Paint or colour the drawing.

FRONT of CARD ~
CLOSED →

CUT AWAY THE
SURPLUS FROM
AROUND THE
TOP of THE
SUN'S DISC.

INSIDE of CARD
~ OPEN →

greetings

Paper angels

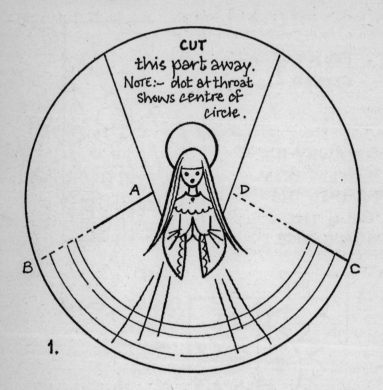

CUT
this part away.
NOTE:— dot at throat
shows centre of
circle.

A   D

B   C

1.

1 Make a circle of paper about 8 cm in diameter and copy the figure above onto it in the proper proportion. Cut away the part you don't want and slit lines AB and CD halfway, one from the top and the other from the bottom as shown by the thicker line.

2 Fold the circle round and slot the notches into each other behind, to make the wings.

2. BACK VIEW.

You can make these out of silver, gold or patterned paper without any features drawn on them — the one drawn left (1), is rather small but would do for this.

Or — draw and colour the design on plain white or coloured paper.

They will stand up or you can attach a thread to the back and hang them up, e.g. on a Christmas tree.

Experiment with different sizes.

Sometimes you can clip the wings, as shown (3), and, if you want, bend them slightly forwards or backwards (4, 5) at the tips.

3.   4.   5.

Matchbox armchair and sofa

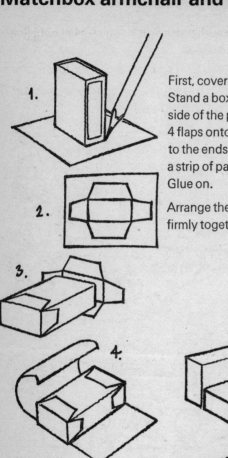

1.

2.

First, cover each box with pretty paper. Stand a box end down on the wrong side of the paper and draw round. Draw 4 flaps onto the 4 sides. Cut out. Glue to the ends of the box. Measure and cut a strip of paper to go round the sides. Glue on.

Arrange the boxes as shown and glue firmly together.

3.

4.

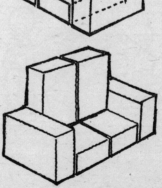

YOU NEED
4 BOXES FOR
A CHAIR AND
6 FOR A
SOFA.

Water prints

Use either waterproof ink or household paint. You also need a shallow dish and some quite absorbent paper.

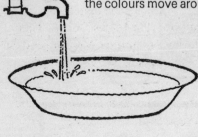

1 Half-fill the dish with water.
2 Drip some drops of ink or paint onto the surface. Let the colours move around into a pattern.

Push it round a bit with a pencil if necessary.
3 Take a piece of paper and lay it flat on the surface of the water for a few seconds.
4 Remove quickly without dragging across the surface and lay it face upwards on newspaper to dry.

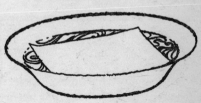

You can change the pattern by gently swirling the water about with a pencil to make a different print.

Slithery fish

Trace the fish on the opposite page onto paper and cut round it to make a pattern. Pin it to some felt or old suede and mark round it with chalk or pencil. Repeat to make the other side of the fish, or cut two from double-thickness material. Use any colour.

Put the two shapes together and sew all round with small, close stitches, sewing *across* the fin and tail following the dotted lines. Leave a small opening underneath between the arrows.

Through the hole fill him with uncooked rice. (You can use cottonwool but it feels more like a real fish with rice.) Sew up the last bit.

Cut out and glue on felt or paper shapes for eyes and side fin. Sit him on a shelf with a few pebbles and shells.

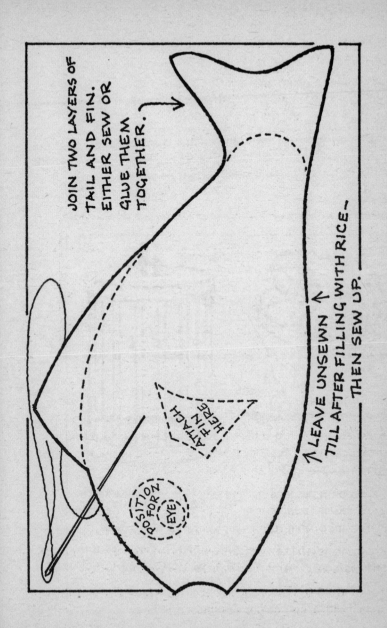

JOIN TWO LAYERS OF TAIL AND FIN. EITHER SEW OR GLUE THEM TOGETHER.

LEAVE UNSEWN TILL AFTER FILLING WITH RICE — THEN SEW UP.

ATTACH FIN HERE

POSITION FOR EYE

Cheese-box bird cage

Cut 2 narrow strips of corrugated paper. Glue them into a round cheese-spread box and its lid.

Collect some drinking-straws, lolly sticks or pieces of wire all the same length. Stick one end into the corrugated paper round the base and the other into the top, glueing firmly.

Make a small loop of a few strands of fuse wire, twist the ends and poke them through a small bead, then through the centre of the cage top, through two holes of a small button and twist together.

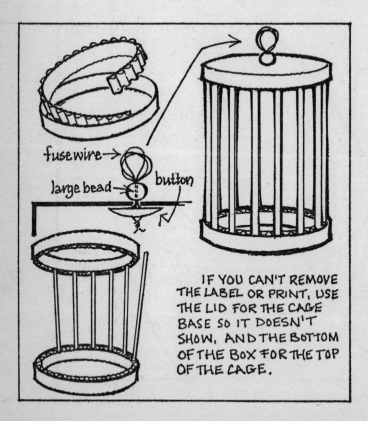

fuse wire →

large bead → button

IF YOU CAN'T REMOVE THE LABEL OR PRINT, USE THE LID FOR THE CAGE BASE SO IT DOESN'T SHOW, AND THE BOTTOM OF THE BOX FOR THE TOP OF THE CAGE.

Fantasy bird

Twist some wire into roughly the shape shown ; make big feet so it will stand up.

Crumple some silver foil and mould it round the wire to make the head and body.

Find a few feathers to twist the wire round for a tail, or cut strips of paper and curl by pulling up between a straight edge and your thumb.

Stick pins on the head for a comb, 2 feathers for wings and drawing-pins for eyes.

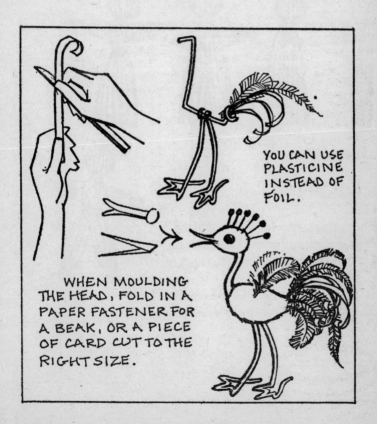

YOU CAN USE PLASTICINE INSTEAD OF FOIL.

WHEN MOULDING THE HEAD, FOLD IN A PAPER FASTENER FOR A BEAK, OR A PIECE OF CARD CUT TO THE RIGHT SIZE.

Wool dolls

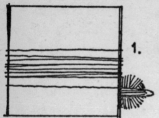

1. Wind some wool round a piece of card several times.
2 Tie wool through the loop at one end and cut through the one at the bottom.

3 Bind wool round near the top to make head and neck.
4 Wind another section of wool round the card, not so thick as the first. Tie both ends and put through the body under the neck for arms.
5 Bind wool round the body for the waist.
6 Separate the wool in half for legs and tie round the ankles.

If you want to do more you can sew on eyes and mouth and add extra wool for hair.

To do this wind a piece of wool round your fingers, tie in the middle, sew to the top of the head and cut the ends.

Dress the dolls with scraps of material, ribbon, tissue paper, or by binding different coloured wools round arms and legs.

Make a jigsaw

Take a large picture from a magazine and paste it smoothly onto thin card. Press flat under a heavy weight until quite dry.

With sharp scissors cut the picture into pieces – it is easier to cut shapes with straight lines as shown. You can rule some lines very lightly to guide you.

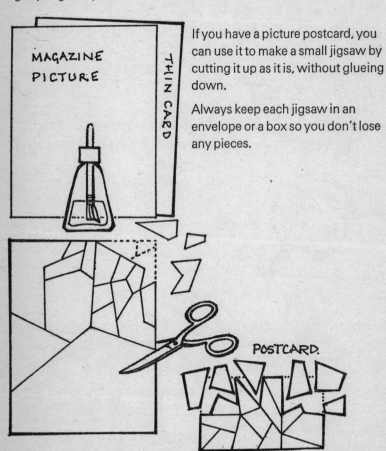

If you have a picture postcard, you can use it to make a small jigsaw by cutting it up as it is, without glueing down.

Always keep each jigsaw in an envelope or a box so you don't lose any pieces.

Flying birds

FOLD

Fold a piece of stiff, brightly coloured paper (or gold or silver paper) in half and draw the bird onto it against the fold where indicated.

Add an eye and any other details you want.

Cut it out and glue the 2 sides of the head together. Do *not* cut along the fold.

Attach a thread of nylon or cotton to each wing.

Spread the wings a little apart and hang up.

Of course you do not have to limit yourself to this size or shape.

Cushion cover with . . .

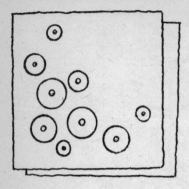

Cut 2 squares the same size of strong, plain material.

They need not be the same colour.

Use tailor's chalk or pastels to draw circles of various sizes in an interesting arrangement on one square. Make a small circle in the centre of each.

Thread some very narrow ribbon into a large darning-needle or bodkin, and, starting with a knot on the wrong side of the material, take big stitches from the centre circle to the outer circle, to form the petals of the flower.

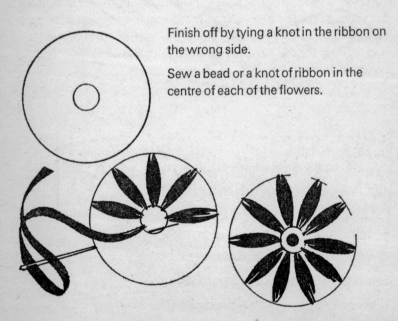

Finish off by tying a knot in the ribbon on the wrong side.

Sew a bead or a knot of ribbon in the centre of each of the flowers.

. . . ribbon embroidery

When you have finished the flowers, place the two squares of material
right sides together and sew all round the edge except for a small gap.
Turn right side out. Stuff with whatever you have on hand, an old
cushion, foam rubber, cut-up rags or old tights, (washed first), and
sew up the last bit of the side.

Matchbox raft

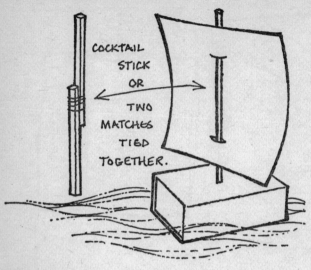

COCKTAIL STICK OR TWO MATCHES TIED TOGETHER.

PAPER SAIL

Cut a sail out of stiff paper, any colour. Make 2 holes to poke a cocktail stick or toothpick through.

Push the end of the stick into the centre of a matchbox. Fix with a dab of glue.

Butterflies

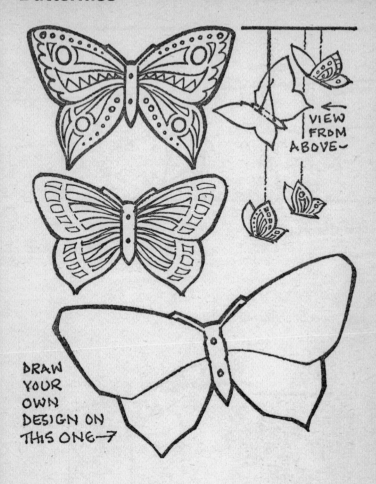

VIEW FROM ABOVE~

DRAW YOUR OWN DESIGN ON THIS ONE—7

Draw or trace the butterfly shape onto stiff brightly coloured paper. Make them bigger if you like. Copy the wing designs or make up your own. Paint them and decorate with sequins or silver 'glitter'. Thread cotton through the holes marked on the body – and tie on the plain side. Bend the wings upwards and hang up.

Make a lantern

You need a piece of stiff paper about 60 cm long and 25 cm wide.

Draw leaf shapes on the paper. 2 designs are shown on this page and the one opposite.

Cut the shapes out neatly.

Glue green cellophane or tissue paper behind the shapes on the wrong side.

wrong side of paper ↰

Put 4 bits of twine through the top of the shade and tie the other ends to a curtain-ring.

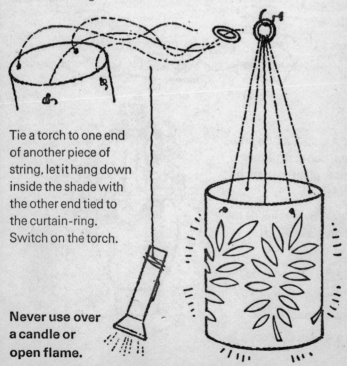

Tie a torch to one end of another piece of string, let it hang down inside the shade with the other end tied to the curtain-ring. Switch on the torch.

Never use over a candle or open flame.

Miniature flower vase

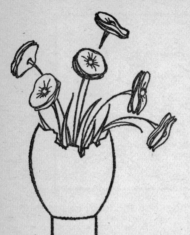

Next time you eat a boiled egg, break it carefully and wash the shell out afterwards.

Cut a strip of stiff paper, fold it into a ring and glue.

Then glue the eggshell into it to make a vase for small flowers.

use white paper, or the same colour as the egg.

GLUE

If you do it very carefully and gently you can plant a very small whole plant in it, such as a wild violet.

Hold it with the root inside the egg and drop a little soil in round the root.

Don't press it down or you might break the egg.

Add a few drops of water.

Building blocks

This is something you can do or make bit by bit.

When you come across small offcuts of wood such as you might find where a carpenter works, or in the rubble from a builder's yard, ask if there are any unwanted scraps of wood. Any shape will do.

First sandpaper them smooth.

Leave some the natural colour. Others can be varnished or given a smooth coat of paint.

Keep your collection in a box and add to it as you find more. When you build with them you will discover which are the most useful shapes.

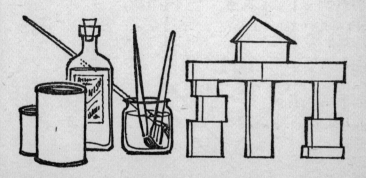

Paper houses . . .

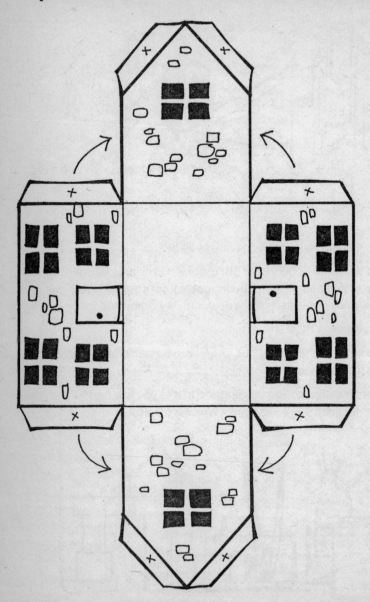

. . . to make a village

Trace the design onto stiff paper.

All except the flaps marked x, must be measured accurately and ruled square. Cut out.

Glue on paper doors and windows or draw them before assembling house.

Bend inwards along all lines on house and chimney except those along flaps marked y, which you bend outwards.

Glue side flaps behind house ends, and glue roof to roof flaps.

Glue chimney together by side flaps marked x, then glue to roof by flaps marked y.

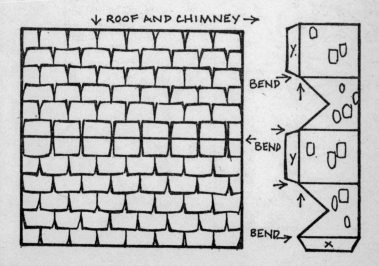

↓ ROOF AND CHIMNEY →

BEND →

← BEND

→

← BEND

→

BEND →

Golden cockerel

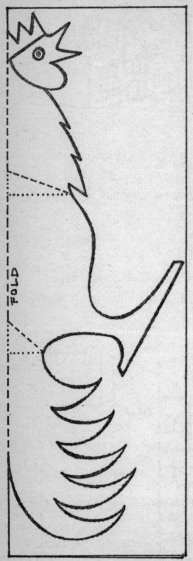

Fold a piece of stiff paper and trace the figure onto one side with the back along the fold.

Cut out through both thicknesses.

Turn the tracing over and draw the lines and head on the blank side.

Fold *up* on the dotted lines and *down* on the dashed ones.

Put a dab of glue between the 2 sides of head and tail.

Colour him yellow and brown.

Cup-and-ball game

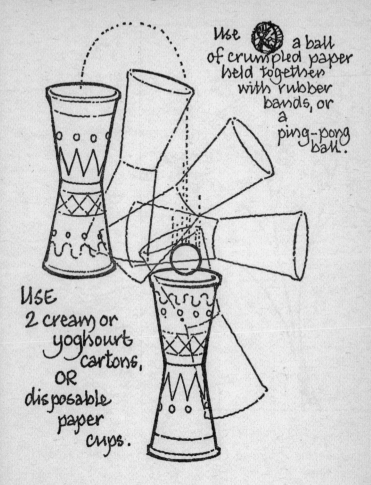

Use a ball of crumpled paper held together with rubber bands, or a ping-pong ball.

USE 2 cream or yoghourt cartons, OR disposable paper cups.

Glue the bottoms of the containers together firmly – decorate them if you like.

To play : hold the cups by the middle in one hand with the ball in the top one. Toss it up and twist the cups quickly so as to catch it in the other one.

'Twiggies'

You need:
a sheet
of
cardboard,
a couple of
thin
pliable
twigs,
glue,
some stiff
paper,
and
paints.

1 Paint the surface of the card. Choose a colour which the twigs will show up against.

2 When the paint is dry, arrange the twigs on the background to make a tree-shape. Glue down firmly.

3 On stiff paper draw some leaves, flowers and birds. Paint them in bright colours. Allow to dry.

4 When dry, cut them out carefully and glue to the 'tree' to make an attractive design. In autumn you could use real leaves if you find some prettily coloured ones.

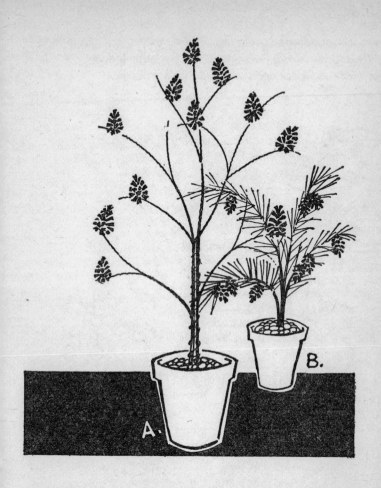

If you'd like your 'twiggies' to be free-standing, as above, fill a flowerpot with earth, clay or pebbles, and stick the twig(s) firmly into it.

Gather some fir-cones and paint them bright colours, or spray them silver or gold. When they're quite dry, fix them to the branches with thin wire, such as fuse wire. Fix them upright on ordinary twigs, as (A) or, if you use evergreens, let them hang downwards, as (B).

Snaky

Collect at least 9 empty cotton reels, the more the better, some large beads if possible and some plain buttons not larger than the reels in diameter. You will also need some thin, strong twine.

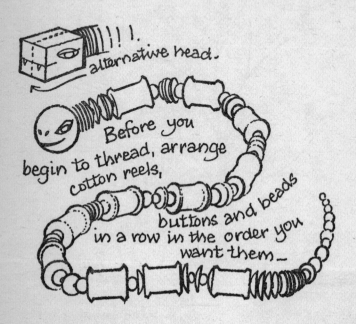

alternative head.

Before you begin to thread, arrange cotton reels, buttons and beads in a row in the order you want them—

Then, starting at the neck end, thread the parts of the snake together. When you get to the tail end, thread the twine all the way back, being sure to use the opposite hole in the buttons this time or they won't be in the centre. Put the twine through the neck end, and tie the 2 pieces of twine together.

The head can be either a ping-pong ball or 2 matchboxes glued together, covered with paper and painted. Glue the head firmly to the last button forming the 'neck'.

Make a notebook

Cut several sheets of paper twice the size you want the notebook to be, or use some sheets of notepaper ready cut. Cut one sheet of thicker paper, preferably coloured, to the same size.

Fold each page accurately in half, also the cover. Place the folded sheets inside each other then inside the cover.

Open out flat keeping neatly in line, and hold with clips while you pierce 3 holes down the middle fold. Use thick thread to sew together through the holes as shown above ; pull up, but not too tightly, and tie the ends in a knot round the thread inside.

STICK OR DRAW A LABEL ON THE COVER.

DECORATE IF YOU LIKE.

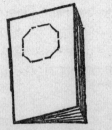

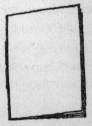

The long and the short of it

Take an empty scouring-powder container and a shorter, fatter one, also of cardboard, to make these characters.

First paint them, or cover with plain paper.

Use black paint or paper for the man's coat and make slits in the sides for arms and ears which are cut from thin card. Make the woman's hair of wool tied in the middle, glued on and fixed in a bun at the back.

Glue on bottle-top noses, a moustache, tie, some 'hair', and draw in eyebrows and mouth.

DRINKING-STRAWS AND WOOL FOR HAIR.

BLACK DRAW in or CUT

PAPER MOUSTACHE.

PAPER EYELASHES AND EYEBROWS

EYES of paper shapes and drawing-pins.

EARS of THIN CARD put through a slit or glue on.

BOTTLE-TOP NOSES.

TIE - a twist of white paper.

TEETH of THIN CARD. put through slit.

FOR ARMS CUT OUT THIN CARD.

cut off one edge of cake-frill for a SKIRT.

Limbs, features and trimmings for the figures.

Decorated jars

Choose empty jars with good lids and use either oil paints or any spare household paint. One colour is enough for a simple design. Wash the labels off the jars first.

Decide what you are going to write or draw and work out the design the size you want it on paper.

Roll the paper and put into the jar facing outwards. Use it as a pattern to trace the design onto the outside, painting it on with a small brush.

Use turpentine or white spirit to wipe off any mistakes and to clean the brush. Use only one colour on the brush at a time.

You can paint the lid to match or just add a design to match the rest.

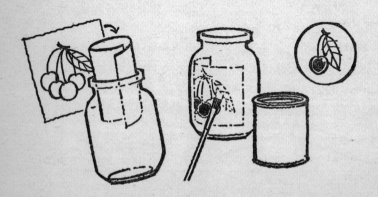

Imitation clock

You can use this for a wall decoration, or to teach a small brother or sister to tell the time. Use the back of a paper plate to make the clock-face. (If you don't have one, cut a circle of card drawn round a plate.) Mark a smaller circle inside it by using a smaller plate or saucer.

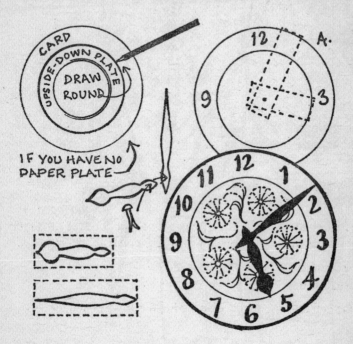

Mark the centre of the circle.

Take two strips of card which will fit the clock-face as shown at A.

Draw, paint and cut out the hour and minute hands, one reaching to the edge and the other to the inner circle.

Paint the numbers, starting with 12, 6, 9 and 3.

Decorate the clock-face with a few flowers.

Put a paper-fastener through the hands, then through the middle of the plate.

Dried leaves and flowers

Dry grasses and flowers in a dark, dry place hung in bunches not tied too closely. Experiment to see which flowers dry best, keeping their colour.

Choose perfect flowers, only just out.

For large flowers, make holes in the side of a grocery box, and poke the stalks through so the heads lay flat on the cardboard.

Leaves and ferns can be dried by laying flat on newspaper under a carpet, with more newspaper between the leaves and the carpet.

Leave for about 3 weeks till dry.

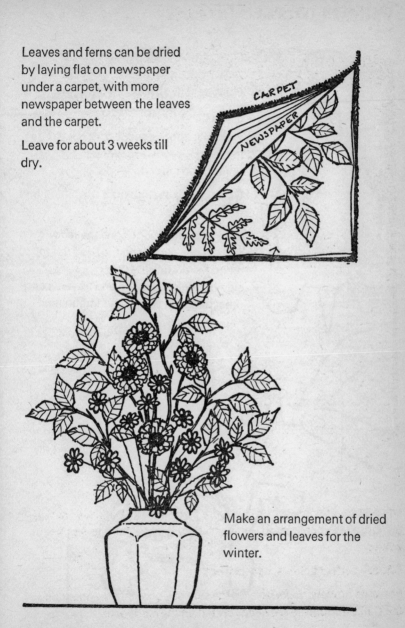

Make an arrangement of dried flowers and leaves for the winter.

Walnut tortoise

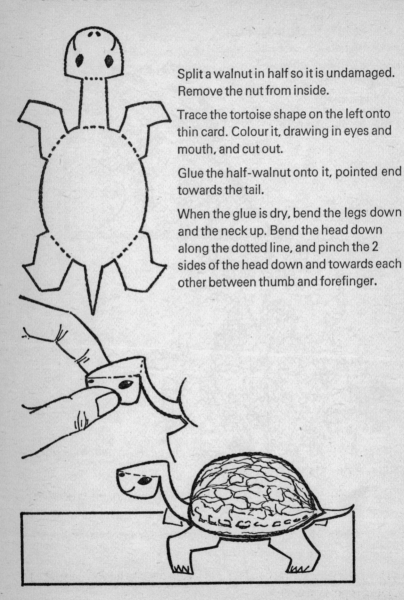

Split a walnut in half so it is undamaged. Remove the nut from inside.

Trace the tortoise shape on the left onto thin card. Colour it, drawing in eyes and mouth, and cut out.

Glue the half-walnut onto it, pointed end towards the tail.

When the glue is dry, bend the legs down and the neck up. Bend the head down along the dotted line, and pinch the 2 sides of the head down and towards each other between thumb and forefinger.

Bead game

YOU NEED: Bottom half of a small box, cardboard the same size as bottoms of box,

4 small round beads, piece of transparent cellophane or acetate.

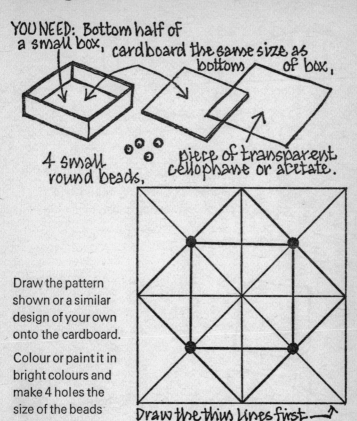

Draw the pattern shown or a similar design of your own onto the cardboard.

Colour or paint it in bright colours and make 4 holes the size of the beads where the dots are.

Draw the thin lines first —➔

If the card is very thin put another layer under it and pierce the holes through both layers.

Put them into the bottom of the box, then the beads, loose, Choose smooth round ones.

Cover the box with cellophane, transparent plastic or acetate, fixed with sticky tape or a rubber band.

The game is to roll the beads round inside the box till you can get all 4 into the holes at once.

73

Potato robots . . .

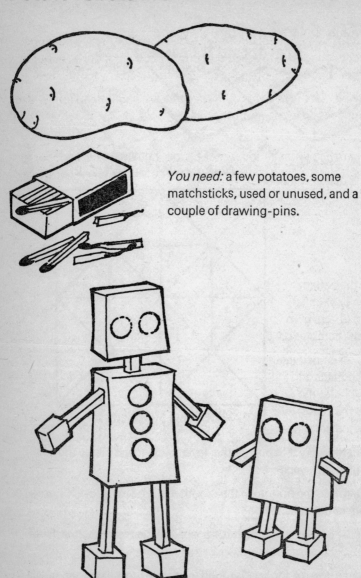

You need: a few potatoes, some matchsticks, used or unused, and a couple of drawing-pins.

. . . and potato animals

Robots
Cut a chunk of potato for the body. Before you stick matchsticks into it for arms, legs and neck, sharpen the *other* ends so it will be easier to push small bits onto them for hands, feet and head.

Cut a chunk for the head and fairly large feet so it will stand firmly. Use drawing-pins for eyes and 'buttons'.

Animals
Put together in the same way as the robots, but use whole matches for the legs. Sharpen *both* ends of small pieces of match for ears and use match-heads for eyes.

Six-wing pin wheel

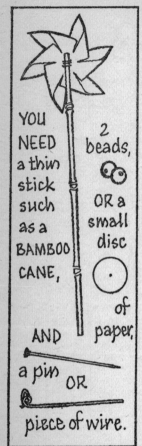

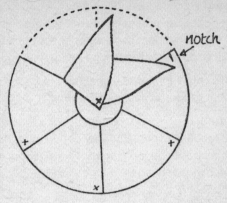

notch

YOU NEED a thin stick such as a BAMBOO CANE,

2 beads,

OR a small disc

of paper,

AND a pin OR piece of wire.

Draw a circle on stiff paper. With the same radius mark off 6 equal sections round the edge.

Draw a small circle in the centre.

Cut lines from the 6 points marked, towards the centre as far as the inner circle.

Fold the left-hand corner of each section to the centre, making a notch, as shown, in the last one to fit it in.

Make a hole through the centre which should pierce each wing.

Thread one bead or the paper disc onto the pin or wire, then put it through the centre hole and add the second bead.

Stick the pin into the stick or wind the wire round.

Beady people

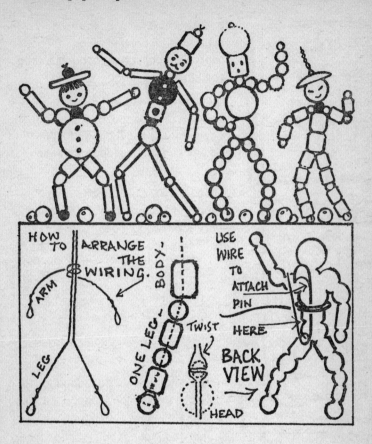

With an assortment of beads and some small buttons you can make a collection of little people. Some ideas are shown, but you can make up your own according to the beads you have.

You can paint eyes, mouth, 'buttons', etc, but for glass beads you would need oil paint and they do quite well without.

For a brooch, use fuse wire (or thread) wound between the beads to fix a safety-pin to the back.

Stand-up figures

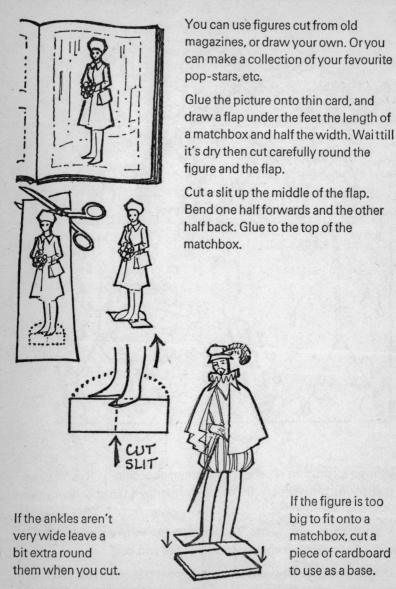

You can use figures cut from old magazines, or draw your own. Or you can make a collection of your favourite pop-stars, etc.

Glue the picture onto thin card, and draw a flap under the feet the length of a matchbox and half the width. Wait till it's dry then cut carefully round the figure and the flap.

Cut a slit up the middle of the flap. Bend one half forwards and the other half back. Glue to the top of the matchbox.

CUT SLIT

If the ankles aren't very wide leave a bit extra round them when you cut.

If the figure is too big to fit onto a matchbox, cut a piece of cardboard to use as a base.

Try drawing your own
people or trace the clown
on this page onto thin
card.

Colour it brightly, cut the
slit in the base and glue
to the matchbox as
before.

Paper flowers

Use coloured crepe or tissue paper.

1 Cut a narrow strip of black paper and clip into a fringe.
2 Take a different colour. Cut a wider and longer strip. Fold into a 'concertina' and cut a petal-shape through all thicknesses.
3 Make a wider strip the same colour. Cut the same way.

Wrap 1 round the end of a wire. Tie with cotton. Wind strips 2 and 3 on top.

Wind a strip of green round the wire from top to bottom. Glue.

Make leaves the same way as petals ; bind in as you cover the stalk.

Picture tiles

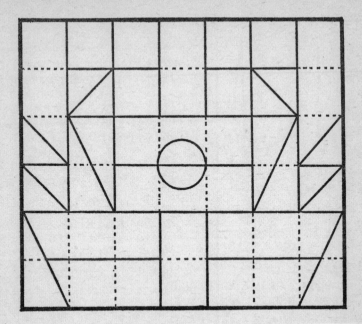

On a piece of thin card or stiff paper 17·5 cm across and 15 cm down mark out 2·5 cm squares.

Copy the pattern above onto it and cut out the shapes neatly. Colour the pieces brightly on both sides with ink or paint of some sort. If they curl, flatten them again when they are dry by putting them under a heavy weight.

Use the shapes to make patterns or pictures.

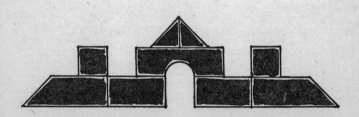

Paper bag faces

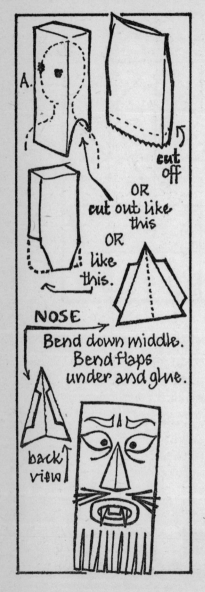

A.

cut off

OR
cut out like
this

OR
like
this.

NOSE

Bend down middle.
Bend flaps
under and glue.

back
view

You can make funny or fantastic faces out of plain, strong, paper bags large enough to go over your head.

Never use plastic or polythene bags, as you can't breathe through them.

Always use loose-fitting, *paper* bags.

Try the paper bag on first; if it is too long either cut it short to fit or cut a piece out at the side. Cut two holes in the appropriate places to see through.

Now you can take it off and decorate it as you wish.

Try the one worn here. With a bag cut as at A, clip the front and back bits into fringes for beard and hair. Draw or paint in the features with poster paints, black ink or felt pens.

Use raffia, wool or hay tied in a bunch to the top for hair. Cut a nose shape, bend down the middle and glue the flaps to the face. Glue on straws or bristles for whiskers.

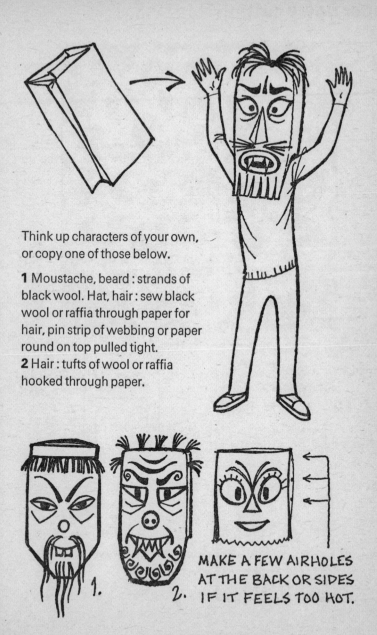

Think up characters of your own, or copy one of those below.

1 Moustache, beard : strands of black wool. Hat, hair : sew black wool or raffia through paper for hair, pin strip of webbing or paper round on top pulled tight.
2 Hair : tufts of wool or raffia hooked through paper.

1.

2. MAKE A FEW AIRHOLES AT THE BACK OR SIDES IF IT FEELS TOO HOT.

Paper doyly cutting

Take a square piece of thin paper and fold it neatly as shown by the dotted lines in figs 1 to 4. The finished shape is shown in fig 5.

With sharp scissors, cut out pieces down the two long sides in a pattern. Cut through all thicknesses.

You can lightly draw the lines you want to cut on the paper first, before cutting away the unwanted parts. Open out carefully.

Kitchen banjo

You need about 4 rubber bands of different sizes, and a small empty carton which they will stretch round.

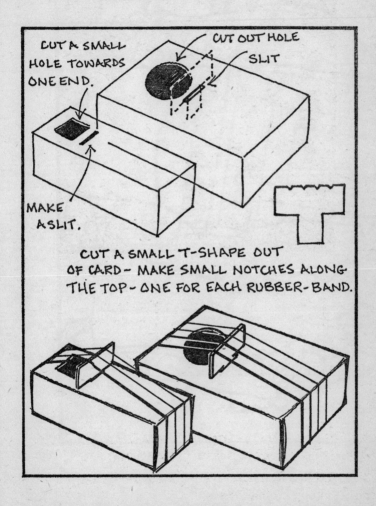

CUT A SMALL HOLE TOWARDS ONE END.

CUT OUT HOLE

SLIT

MAKE A SLIT.

CUT A SMALL T-SHAPE OUT OF CARD — MAKE SMALL NOTCHES ALONG THE TOP — ONE FOR EACH RUBBER-BAND.

Pluck the strings gently so as not to break the bands. The different sizes will give differently pitched notes.

Standing elephant

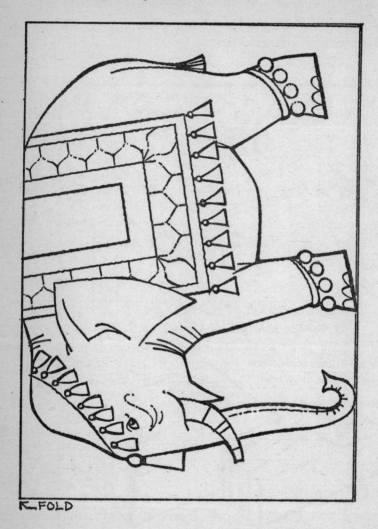

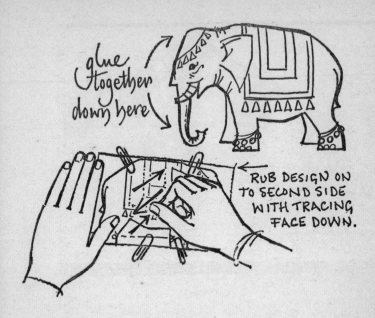

glue together down here

RUB DESIGN ON TO SECOND SIDE WITH TRACING FACE DOWN.

You need a piece of stiff paper the size drawn on the opposite page when it's folded in half, with the fold along the longest side.

Trace this drawing onto one side with the elephant's back along the fold.

Paint or colour the elephant grey, and his ornaments in bright colours.

Cut out all round the drawing leaving the back joined along the fold.

Stick the front of the head and the trunk together.

Pull the legs apart and press the back down slightly and the elephant will stand up by itself.

Paint the second side too if you like, by placing your tracing face down on the blank side, fixing with paper clips and rubbing the design down with your thumb nail.

'Flagging'

Make a string of flags to decorate your room, or in miniature for the Christmas tree.

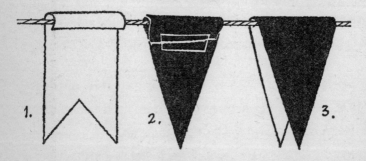

1. 2. 3.

With paper coloured on both sides, cut as 1 and 2, and fold tops over the string using glue or sticky tape to fix.

With paper only coloured on one side, cut flag double as shown at 3.

'Snapdragon'

1 Take a piece of paper about 12 cm square.
2 Crease in half.
3 Fold outside edges to the crease.
4 Fold along the first crease.
5 Bend over 1 cm of each top edge outwards and cut a notch halfway along each edge.
6 Bend over the corners each end as shown and tuck under one folded edge.
7 Open it out at the centre and snap the ends together so it looks like a mouth.
8 Paint on eyes, nose, mouth, etc. Glue in a red tongue. Use *thin* paper so as not to prevent the mouth closing.

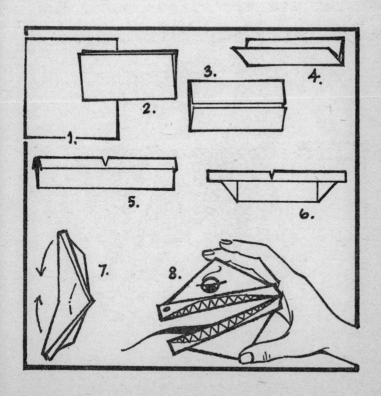

Acorn-cup man

You need 2 long pieces of thread to go up through the legs, body and head, and 2 shorter pieces for the arms.

Collect some acorn-cups for the figure and one for the head with the acorn still in it. Put aside the bigger ones, if sizes vary, to use for the body.

Cut some circles of coloured paper, 3 large for the neck frill and 12 smaller ones for sleeves and trousers.

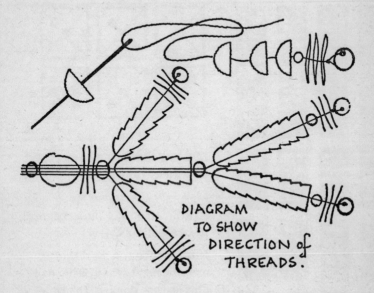

DIAGRAM
TO SHOW
DIRECTION of
THREADS.

Tie a large bead onto the end of each thread.

Use a needle to thread 3 paper frills onto one of the long bits of cotton, a small bead, then enough acorn-cups for the leg. Do the same for the second leg. Put both pieces of cotton through the needle at once and thread a bead, the cups for the body, another bead, the 3 large paper circles and finally the head. Add a bead on top, then make a knot in the cotton close to the head.

Thread the arms the same way. You can either put these strings through the head too or tie them to the others under the neck frills. Make a loop with the spare cotton at the top.

A set of dominoes

It's best to use thin black card, but any colour will do – even white, when you can draw the dots in black.

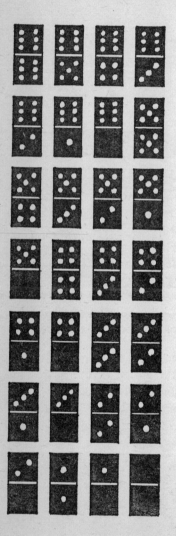

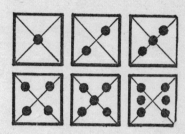

Measure and cut out 28 pieces of card 2·5 cm by 5 cm.

Make sure the corners are square. With a ruler draw a line across each piece exactly halfway.

Now, as shown in the diagrams, mark the number and position of dots on each domino. Then mark in the spots and line across the middle in ink, paint or felt pen, white on black, or black on white or coloured card.

Coin rubbings

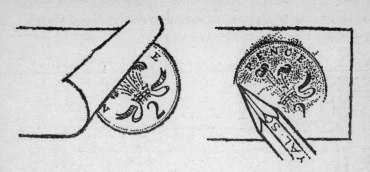

Make a collection of copies of coins of all sorts. Begin with British ones and then add foreign ones and old coins.

You can borrow interesting coins and return them when you have made a copy, as it won't hurt them.

Cut out the best impressions. Glue them into a book without smudging them.

The way to do it : Place the coin under a piece of thin white paper and hold it firmly while you rub gently over the surface of the coin through the paper, using the side of the lead of a fairly soft pencil. If you can't hold it steady, fix the underside of the coin to the table with sticky tape.

Bottle and paper aquarium

Find as large a glass jar as you can, such as a preserving jar, sweet jar or one that has held coffee, as long as you can see through it.

1 Put a piece of crumpled tissue or brown paper into the bottom to look like rocks or sand.

2 Cut coloured paper into seaweed shapes. Fix to the inside of the jar, held either by the paper base or a dab of glue.

3 Cut out starfish and glue them to paper 'rocks'.
4 Cut fish shapes out of coloured paper. If it's only coloured one side, fold it and cut double as both sides will show.

Paint or draw on eyes, etc, and tie thread to hang it up by. Put the other end through a piece of card cut to the inside size of the jar lid, on threads of different lengths. Some lids have card already inside which you can use.

Put the card on top of the jar with the fish dangling inside. If you can, replace the jar lid to hold them in place.

Paper boat

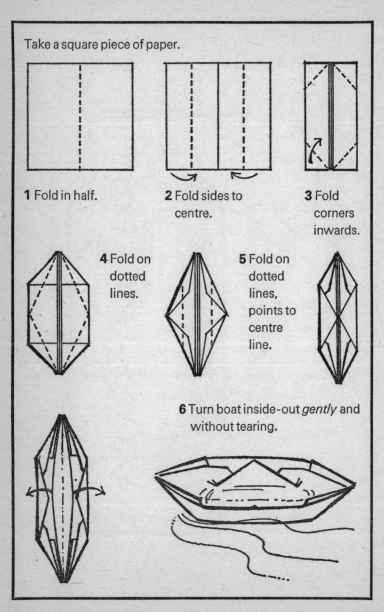

Take a square piece of paper.

1 Fold in half.

2 Fold sides to centre.

3 Fold corners inwards.

4 Fold on dotted lines.

5 Fold on dotted lines, points to centre line.

6 Turn boat inside-out *gently* and without tearing.

Home-made dice

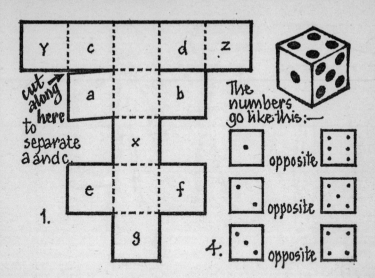

Copy diagram 1 above very carefully onto stiff paper. It is easier if you make it fairly large, with the squares about 2·5 cm each way.

Cut between squares a and c, and b and d.

Bend along all the dotted lines.

Fold up a and b, also e, f and g, then roll upwards along the middle row of squares so e and f cover a and b. (2)

Wrap the last strip round the cube, tucking y and z into the slits each side of square x. (3)

Paint on the spots (4). Use a container large enough to shake the dice about in.

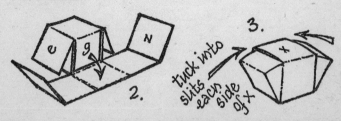

Wire dolls

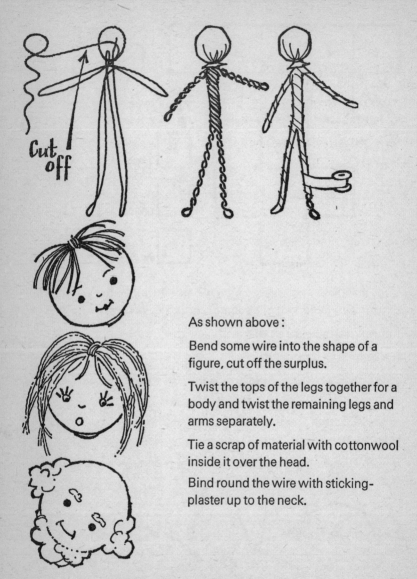

Cut off

As shown above:

Bend some wire into the shape of a figure, cut off the surplus.

Twist the tops of the legs together for a body and twist the remaining legs and arms separately.

Tie a scrap of material with cottonwool inside it over the head.

Bind round the wire with sticking-plaster up to the neck.

Dress the doll with scraps of material glued, sewn or tied on (blouse, skirt, apron, scarf, shirt and dress).

Paint or sew on eyes, nose and mouth.

Glue or sew on wool or cottonwool for hair.

Bind legs with coloured wool for stockings or trousers.

Trim a matchstick or twig for a walking-stick.

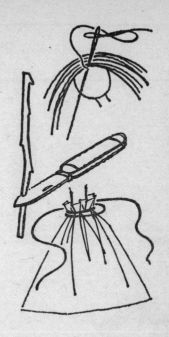

Illusion

BEND IN HALF ALONG DOTTED LINE

From a plain white postcard cut a piece the size shown on the opposite page and trace pony and cart onto it exactly in the position shown.

Colour or paint the drawings.

Fold the card in half along the dotted line, punch holes each side where crosses are drawn and thread a short string through each.

Twirl the card between thumbs and forefingers of both hands and it will look as if the pony is harnessed to the cart.

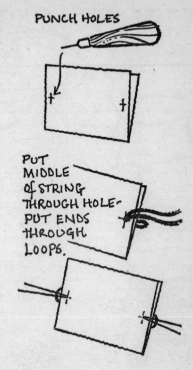

PUNCH HOLES

PUT MIDDLE of STRING THROUGH HOLE. PUT ENDS THROUGH LOOPS.

Conker furniture

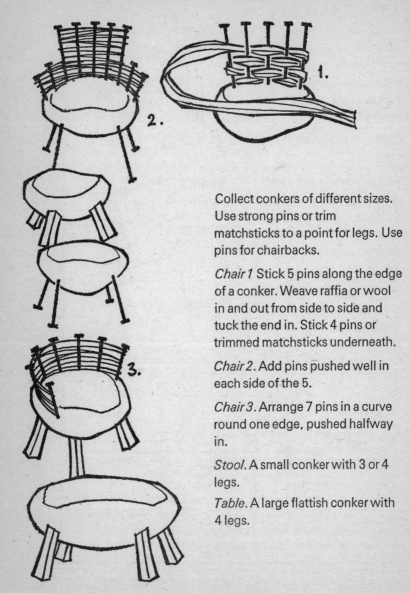

Collect conkers of different sizes. Use strong pins or trim matchsticks to a point for legs. Use pins for chairbacks.

Chair 1 Stick 5 pins along the edge of a conker. Weave raffia or wool in and out from side to side and tuck the end in. Stick 4 pins or trimmed matchsticks underneath.

Chair 2. Add pins pushed well in each side of the 5.

Chair 3. Arrange 7 pins in a curve round one edge, pushed halfway in.

Stool. A small conker with 3 or 4 legs.

Table. A large flattish conker with 4 legs.

Doll's acorn teaset

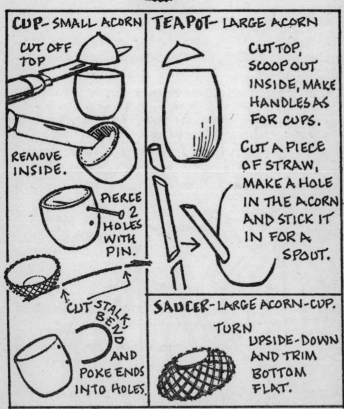

CUP– SMALL ACORN

CUT OFF TOP

REMOVE INSIDE.

PIERCE 2 HOLES WITH PIN.

CUT STALK, BEND AND POKE ENDS INTO HOLES.

TEAPOT– LARGE ACORN

CUT TOP, SCOOP OUT INSIDE, MAKE HANDLES AS FOR CUPS.

CUT A PIECE OF STRAW, MAKE A HOLE IN THE ACORN AND STICK IT IN FOR A SPOUT.

SAUCER– LARGE ACORN–CUP.

TURN UPSIDE-DOWN AND TRIM BOTTOM FLAT.

Paper decorations

You need some sheets of coloured paper.

With a compass draw 8 or 10 circles of the same size on the wrong side of the paper and cut out.

Fold in half with the right side inward.

Glue two folded pieces together by laying the wrong sides together.

Add another and continue till half the circles are stuck together. Do the same with the remaining half.

Glue a loop of string to the centre of one side and join the 2 halves together.

Make small ones for Christmas tree decorations or a large one to hang anywhere.

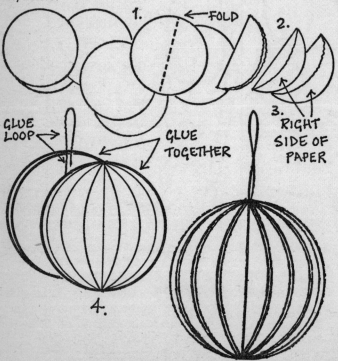

1. ←FOLD

2.

3. RIGHT SIDE OF PAPER

GLUE LOOP→

GLUE TOGETHER

4.

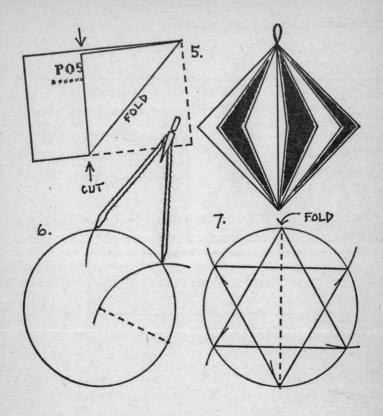

On the same principle you can make one using a square shape instead of the circle. For a small one use a postcard as a pattern to cut round by folding diagonally as fig 5.

For the star draw a circle and with the same radius mark off 6 points round the circle.

Join as shown in fig 7 and cut out the star.

Finish off in the same way as before.

You can use 2 or more different colours for the same decoration arranged as you like, half-and-half, or alternate pieces.

'Making eyes'

CUT SLITS WIDER THAN THE STRIP TO GO THROUGH THEM.

Draw the face on a piece of white card. Cut out the eyeholes. Cut a slit down each side of the card level with the eyes.

Cut a strip of card long enough to stick out each side of the paper, and wider than the eyes.

Slip the strip through the slits behind the eyeholes. Draw on it 2 eyes in the middle of the eyeholes.

Now slide the strip sideways or up and down and make her roll her eyes.

Make a bean-bag

How to play catch without a ball !

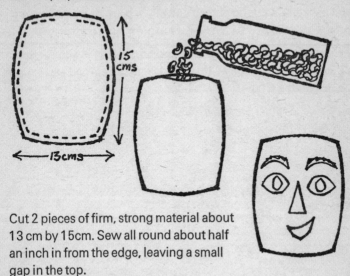

Cut 2 pieces of firm, strong material about 13 cm by 15cm. Sew all round about half an inch in from the edge, leaving a small gap in the top.

Turn the other side out.

Half fill with dried beans.

Sew up hole.

Decorate if you like with bits of felt glued on.

Doll's horse

Use 2 small cardboard boxes and one much larger one (e.g. cereal or detergent packets). Cover them with paper, or paint them, adding a little detergent to the paint if the box is too greasy to cover properly.

Make holes through one side near top and bottom of the large carton. Poke a skewer through each, with a cotton reel on one end and a piece of cork stuck onto the point.

Glue the boxes together as shown. Glue or thread through string or raffia for a tail. Add decorations with paint or glued-on paper.

YOU CAN MAKE HIM WITHOUT THE 'WHEELS' BUT THEY HELP TO GIVE A FIRM BASE.

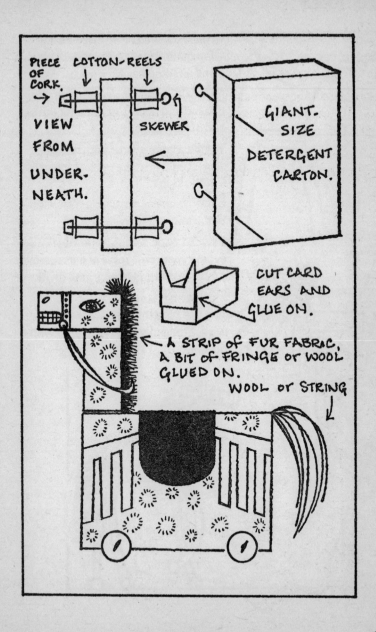

PIECE OF CORK.

COTTON-REELS

SKEWER

VIEW FROM UNDER. NEATH.

GIANT. SIZE DETERGENT CARTON.

CUT CARD EARS AND GLUE ON.

A STRIP OF FUR FABRIC, A BIT OF FRINGE or WOOL GLUED ON.

WOOL or STRING

Wire horse

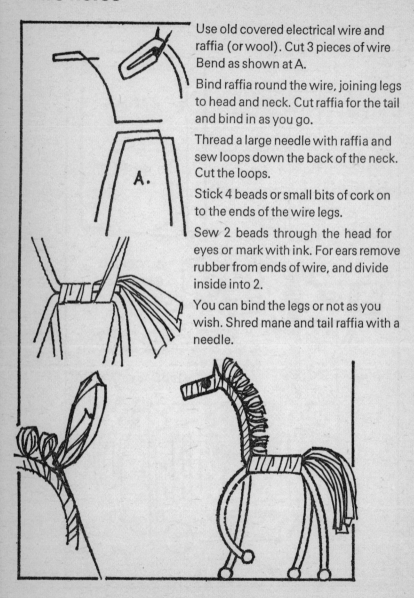

Use old covered electrical wire and raffia (or wool). Cut 3 pieces of wire Bend as shown at A.

Bind raffia round the wire, joining legs to head and neck. Cut raffia for the tail and bind in as you go.

Thread a large needle with raffia and sew loops down the back of the neck. Cut the loops.

Stick 4 beads or small bits of cork on to the ends of the wire legs.

Sew 2 beads through the head for eyes or mark with ink. For ears remove rubber from ends of wire, and divide inside into 2.

You can bind the legs or not as you wish. Shred mane and tail raffia with a needle.

A.

Leaf rubbings

Lay a leaf upside-down on paper or card and glue down if you have difficulty holding it still while rubbing.

Take a piece of white paper, thin but strong, and a good quality wax crayon.

Hold the paper over the leaf without letting it move while you rub the paper surface gently with the crayon, in the same direction all the time.

You can experiment with more than one colour.

You can then cut out the leaf shape and stick it in a book or make designs on paper with several leaves.

CHOOSE LEAVES WITH INTERESTING VEIN PATTERNS.

Matchstick designs

Cut off the burnt part of all the used matches you can find – keep them in a jamjar till you have quite a lot.

If you have some waterproof ink you can colour some of the matchsticks. Keep only one colour in a jar. Paint the ink on or dilute in a saucer, dip matches in and lay on newspaper to dry.

Take a piece of stiff paper or thin card, any colour except white.

Work out a design or picture with the matchsticks. Use them as a mass as well as for outlines.

When they are arranged to your liking, pick up each match, add a dab of glue to one side and press gently into place.

Draw or paint in details if you want to, and add paper shapes as suggested opposite.

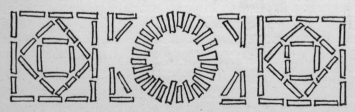

EXPERIMENT FIRST WITH DIFFERENT EFFECTS and PATTERNS BEFORE YOU GLUE THEM DOWN.

Shell mice

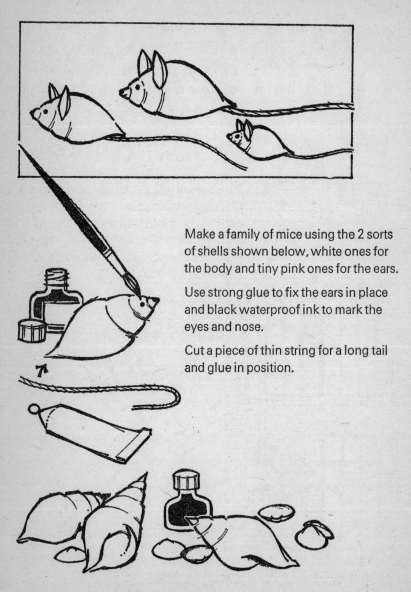

Make a family of mice using the 2 sorts of shells shown below, white ones for the body and tiny pink ones for the ears.

Use strong glue to fix the ears in place and black waterproof ink to mark the eyes and nose.

Cut a piece of thin string for a long tail and glue in position.

Paper windmill

Use the empty tube from a toilet roll. Paint a few windows, railings and doors round it.

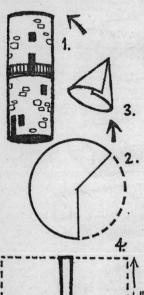

Draw a circle about 10 cm in diameter on stiff paper. Cut out about a third of it, and glue the piece left into a cone which will fit the top of the tube.

From a piece of stiff paper 15 cm square, cut the sails as shown.

Take a small nail, put it through the centre of the sails, through a bead or tiny roll of paper, push it into the tube near the top and stick a bit of cork on the end to hold it. Now glue the cone onto the top of the tube.

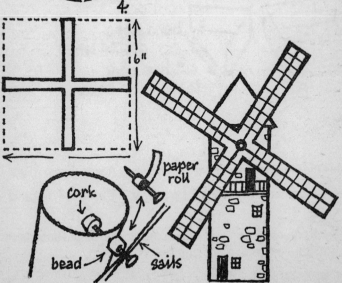

6"

cork

paper roll

bead

sails

Matchbox ship

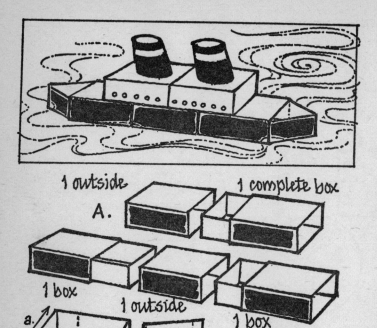

1 outside   1 complete box

A.

1 box   1 outside

a.

1 box

bend along
dotted lines

b.

cut this edge
to width of boxes.

B.   C.

Assemble the required matchboxes as shown at A.

Push them together and glue the 2 top ones to the centre of the other 3.

Cut off the 2 corners of a drawer as indicated by the dotted lines, at B. Sides a and b should be of equal length.

Clip as shown at C.

Bend the side bits inwards slightly along the dotted lines.

Put a dab of glue on the outside of each flap and along the underside of the edge between them. Push the pieces into each end of the boat.

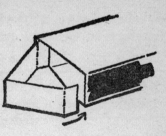

PATTERN for
FUNNEL
Cut 2 if you want
2 funnels.

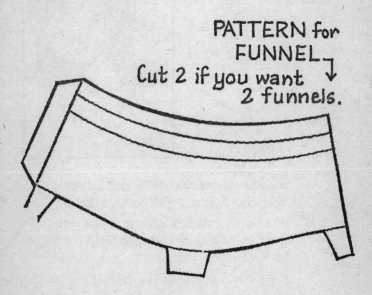

Trace the funnel shape onto stiff paper.

Cut out, including the flaps. Glue into funnel-shape by the side flaps.

Bend bottom flaps outwards. Glue funnel to the top matchboxes. You can make 1 or 2 funnels.

If you have some waterproof paint, e.g. household paint or Indian ink, you can paint the deck white and the sides and funnels black.

Shell necklace

Collect enough shells, and, if they vary in size, grade them with the largest in the middle of the row and the smallest at each end, as at A.

A

Scrape or bore a small hole in each with a pointed instrument. If you're using half-shells, you only need to make 1 hole in each, as in B ; then, using thin string or twine, start at 1 end of the row and knot each shell to secure it as you go along, as in C. If you're using whole shells, then you'll have to

C.

B.

make a hole either side of the pointed end, so your thread can pass straight through, as below.

When the necklace is as long as you want it (make sure that it will fit over your head !) tie the ends of the thread firmly together.

You can of course use all kinds of different shells for your necklace.

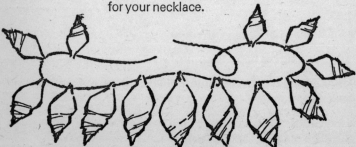

Paper star

Use coloured, white, gold or silver card or thick paper.

Cut 5 strips 2 cm wide and 16 cm long. Bend in half. Cut slits where shown exactly halfway across the width of the card.

Cut a strip 2 cm wide and 24 cm long, divide into 6 equal parts, and bend across the divisions all in the same direction. Clip slits each side of every bend, as shown.

Glue the first section to the last. Using a needle, fix a thread through a bend.

Take the short pieces and slot each one into one side of the 5-sided shape.

Add a dab of glue if they tend to slip out.

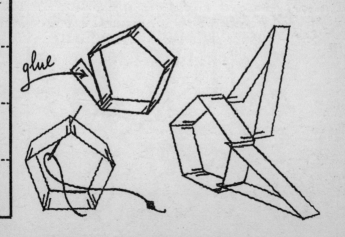

glue

Make a scarecrow

PUT a few FLOWERS in his HAT, REAL or ARTIFICIAL.

STICK HIM FIRMLY INTO THE GROUND TO SCARE AWAY THE BIRDS.

Begin by tying together 2 sticks in a cross shape for arms and body.

The head can be a large swede or turnip with a hole to fix the neck into. Otherwise fill a piece of material with rags and tie it together round the neck.

Fix straw or raffia and an old hat to the head – either sew it or fix with wire and small nails.

If you have some straw tie it round the body and arms to give bulk, but it will do without. An old shirt will clothe him – add a few colourful patches and cut the sleeves ragged. Or you can make a simple shirt with an old bit of cloth.

Fix or pin felt or paper eyes, etc, or cut them into the vegetable – add a scarf.

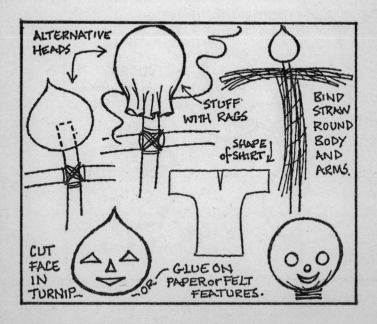

Fruit-skin candles

If you have the remains of some old candles, put them in an old pan and heat gently. Remove the old wicks.

Cut the top off an orange as shown, and spoon out the inside without damaging the skin.

Find an old oil-lamp wick or white shoelace.

Cut a circle of card. Thread wick through centre. Knot. Thread the other end through the orange base and knot the very end of it.

Pour in melted wax. Pull card flat to top of the orange by the end of the wick — and leave till the wax has set hard, before removing it.

PULL TIGHT

After lighting your candle, always watch the flame and be ready to blow it out if it burns too fiercely or causes smoke.

Here's an idea for a hanging candle: first, spoon out the inside of half a grapefruit without damaging the skin.

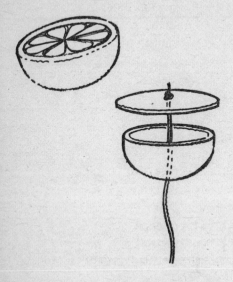

Cut card with a wick through as for the orange, melt candles and pour into grapefruit. Cut 2 long bits of wire, wind together at the middle, bend into shape round the grapefruit as shown, and tie the 4 ends together at the top. Ask an adult to hang it up somewhere safe, away from draughts. You could also cut 4 shorter pieces of wire and put one end of each through the edge of the fruit.

You can use a nightlight standing in the half-grapefruit and orange rather than make your own candles, if you prefer.

If you have enjoyed this Piccolo book,
you may like to choose your next book from
the titles listed on the following pages

More non-fiction from Piccolo

Everyday Inventions 35p
Meredith Hooper

From Coca-Cola and the zip to the sewing machine and television, nearly everything we use has been invented by someone somewhere . . .

First Feats 25p
Peter Tunsall

Lindberg, Hillary, Magellan, Bell, Leonov – these men all achieved a 'first' in their chosen field. 78 exciting stories are told in this lively anthology.

**Piccolo Book of
Amazing Scientific Facts** 25p
Jane Sherman

Do you know . . .
That there is a metal which will melt in your hand?
How a camel stores water inside its body?
What is the fastest-moving creature in the world?
What makes a cobra dance?
Answers to these and many other amazing scientific facts are given in this fascinating book.

Non-fiction
Elizabeth Gundry

Collecting Things 40p

Exciting and practical ideas on how to start over 100
collections; none of them are expensive and none take
up too much room. Clear instructions for the best ways
of arranging your collection and plenty of useful
addresses.

Growing Things 25p

A useful and enthusiastic gardening book for an
absolute beginner — with hints on growing attractive
plants from everyday fruits and vegetables, and
instructions on how to make underwater gardens,
hanging baskets and window boxes.

Making Decorations 25p

A simple, instructive and readable handbook on making
decorations out of everyday things for Christmas,
Easter, birthday parties and Hallowe'en.

Make Your Own Monster 25p

Simple instructions for making monsters of all kinds,
from dressing up as a ghost, to making a dragon mask,
a bat mobile or an abominable snowman.

Sewing Things 25p

The reader is taken step by step through the first stages
of sewing and presented with ideas of things to make,
clearly and practically explained.

Non-fiction

Encyclopedia of Useful Facts 40p
Jean Stroud

A fascinating book annually revised, with literally
thousands of facts on all subjects ranging from the
Solar System and Wonders of Nature to Religion and
the Arts.

Piccolo Encyclopedia of Sport 40p
Peter Mathews

A comprehensive and up-to-date record of the world's
major sporting events, their history and organization,
results and records.

Piccolo All-The-Year-Round Book 50p
Deborah Manley

Festivals and holidays; things to make and do month by
month.

Secrets of the Gypsies 25p
Kay Henwood

A lively account of the customs, rituals and magic of
the Romany gypsy, that will fascinate children of about
eight upwards.

These and other Piccolo books are obtainable from all booksellers
and newsagents. If you have any difficulty please send
purchase price plus 7p postage to

PO Box 11 Falmouth Cornwall

While every effort is made to keep prices low, it is sometimes
necessary to increase prices at short notice. Piccolo Books reserve
the right to show new retail prices on covers which may differ
from those previously advertised in the text or elsewhere.